Since He Walked on Water
We Can Wade Through Life

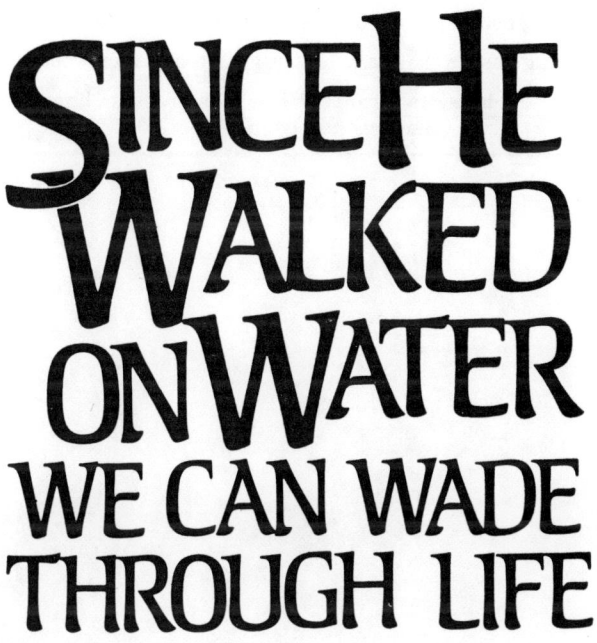

SINCE HE WALKED ON WATER WE CAN WADE THROUGH LIFE

TERRY RUSH

HOWARD PUBLISHING CO.

3117 North 7th
West Monroe, Louisiana 71291

> The purpose of Howard Publishing is threefold:
> ***Inspiring** holiness in the lives of believers,
> ***Instilling** hope in the hearts of struggling people everywhere,
> ***Instructing** believers toward a deeper faith in Jesus Christ,
>   **Because he's coming again.**

© 1991 by Howard Publishing Co., Inc.
All rights reserved.

No part of this publication may be reproduced in any form without the prior written permission of the publisher.

Howard Publishers
3117 North 7th Street, West Monroe, LA 71291-2227

Printed in the United States of America

Second Printing 1991

ISBN# 1-878990-03-9

This Material Is Stolen

I want you to know up front that the contents of this book are not original. I spend much time in study. My heart is continually renewed, reframed, and remolded by the adequate instruction of others. For the influence of all who have donated to my thinking, I am most grateful.

Ideas in this writing came from sources too numerous to mention. I am unable to retrace my thinking processes to recall who said what to give me all my information.

I do know that Chuck Swindoll, through his masterpiece, *Improving Your Serve,* has opened a window to life for me. I thank God for his sensitivity toward the loveliness of serving. And my dear friend, Jim McGuiggan, has had a tremendous impact on my heart. Much of this book has the breath of Jim in it.

To all, especially Chuck and Jim, thank you for your depth of heart which has helped me see the Christ as I had never seen Him before.

Terry Rush

Acknowledgement

Thanks to a host of friends who gave of themselves that this publication might exist. To my dear friends, Ernest and Erin Gammon, thank you for information about World Bible School.

Gayle Yates and Barbara Thrasher and several of the GCCA crew are appreciated for their interest and aid. Linda Jones, Jeanine Jones, Debbie Moore, Shirley English, Kyla Keesee, and Deanna Tipton spent time in finalizing the manuscript.

Thanks to each of you for your labor of love.

Contents

Introduction		ix
Preface		xi
1	What If I Have Short Ankles (Wading by Faith)	1
2	Captured by Enemy Pirates (Wading With Hope)	10
3	No Longer Driven by Winds and Waves (Wading With Maturity)	17
4	Handling the Insalts of Life (Wading With Mercy)	25
5	I'm Going in Over My Head (Wading Through Suffering)	34
6	Buried at Sea (Wading in Obedience)	42
7	Dare to Wade! (Wading With Motivation)	51
Test Time		61

Dedication

This work is dedicated to the first graduating class of Green Country Christian Academy.

Aguilar, Deborah Jean
Allison, Linda
Ashley, Denda Kay
Busby, Cindy Lois
Doke, Marvin Douglas
Eaves, Vickie Marie
Friday, Bridget Lynne
Garner, Clayton William
Gilley, Cynthia Marie
Hunter, Shawna Renee
Kelly, Kathleen Jean
Kinsey, James Dexter
Knight, Larry Gene
McClure, Keith Dwayne
Parrott, David Allen
Preston, Charles Eric
Riggs, Robert Edwin
Vaughn, Lesli
VanDyke, Jeffrey Scott

Never, never, never lose heart!
          Hebrews 12:3

            Terry Rush

Introduction

Christ's walking on water during the storm wasn't a little "party piece" to impress some fawning audience. This astounding miracle was the act of the sovereign Lord manifesting his credentials. But *the occasion* of the miracle was a howling storm threatening a group of frightened and needy disciples.

It's interesting that the Lord permitted his followers to be caught in the storm. His disciples aren't promised exemption from the fearful or frightening. He doesn't show favoritism, not even with his own. His own life was one of the most troubled ever lived, and the disciple is not above his Master. It is enough that the disciple be as his Lord. This is Terry's presupposition as he writes his little book about the challenges he, you, and I face in life.

But why trials, challenges, and storms? Someone said that if the world's most brilliant artist were idly doing a sketch to amuse some child, he would put up with much less than his best. But ask him to do what will represent his life's work, his crowning achievement, and watch how he goes to work. He would pour his whole soul into it, and with much care, toil, and determination would pursue his goal. Nothing would be too much trouble to insure that his creation bore the image of his care and love and brilliance. To ask him not to go to so much trouble would be an insult.

And do you think mankind is the product of God's idle moments? You are God's "masterpiece" and he *will* go to any length to perfect you. Don't ask him to be less conscientious in his molding of you than he is, for that would be asking him to love you less, not more!

Thank God that Christ doesn't leave us out in the storm, but comes to us—cheering us on. Not demanding of us what we *can't* give or be. No, he *alone* is flawless. And while we can't walk on water, we are enabled to honorably "wade through life." And *that's* what Mr. Rush wants to say to us in this book.

Jim McGuiggan

Preface

I have spent far too many years waiting for other people to improve so that I could finally be happy.

When we are self-centered, we believe that the road to happiness is to blame others for our sadness. Then, when Scripture indicates that we need to make a personal adjustment, we can always find an easy excuse as to why it doesn't apply to us . . . this time!

We Can Wade Through Life is written to point the way to real hope and real life—even in the midst of bitter storms. Too many have ground down to a slow drag because they misunderstand servanthood. Others have already quit—pointing the accusing finger at a neighbor or preacher or tragedy.

This book will encourage you to turn dread into hope, hate into love, and disappointment into advancement. As Jesus draws us to the cross, He pulls us deeper into "worthwhile" suffering. As we progress in suffering, we understand how it is possible to get a clearer grasp of "consider it all joy." Once we get hold of this concept, we possess the ability to survive the storm.

No longer will we seek ways to avoid and dissolve rugged trials. While we take up the cross, we will grow to the conclusion that each piercing nail is for the benefit of ourselves and others.

The promise of happiness is registered in the beatitudes (Matt. 5:3-12). The road to that promise is in direct conflict with the academic excellence of the world. Jesus promises that those who are happy are the broken down (v. 3), the mourning (v. 4), the ones who don't walk over people to get where they are going (v. 5), those who crave God's way (v. 6), those who love their opponents (v. 7), those who deny the privileges of pride (v. 8), those who aren't out to do their own thing or stand for their rights (v. 9), and those who can be glad when they are insulted by life's unfairness. These are the ones who can wade!

It's time we got up from the pits of constant, gnawing difficulties. By God's grace, we will discover that those hurts are only invisible band-aids for someone else's healing. *Use your life. Don't be used by life.*

Terry Rush
747 South Memorial
Tulsa, Oklahoma 74112

CHAPTER ONE

What If I Have Short Ankles?
(Wading by Faith)

Is the concept of Jesus practical? Did He and does He exist? Or have many fallen for a "religious crutch" that is a dead-end alley? While contemplating the reality of spiritual existence, we may find that the uninvited guest of doubt continually knocks at our mind's door. "Will there be life after the grave?" "Am I merely psyching myself up for good mental health?" On and on, doubt raises its ugly head.

Is it wise to think that Jesus is real? This book is not written to prove that Jesus is "factual and actual." By faith, we know He is. Ninety percent of all we know is by faith. I have never been to Moscow, but I know it exists. I never met George Washington; however, there is enough evidence to cause me to "believe" he was real.

This book is to help believers, and those who want to believe, to grow in the understanding that Jesus is not a remote "vagueness." He is not distant; He is very near. He is not irrelevant; He is very applicable to us and our daily routines. He is not boring. Furthermore, He never called His followers to be a bunch of down-in-the-mouth deadbeats with their noses stuck up in the air because they went to church so many Sundays without missing. He came that you and I could have more life than we would know how to use (John 10:10). Such abundant life is available! Let us be on our way then!

What robs us of real living? One factor is our inability and unwillingness to "forget." Relationships are no longer close because something awful happened, and one or several will not forget it. Bad experiences of the past fuel doubt's flame. Some never give God an honest chance because they cannot forget what some preacher once did. Others will not enter the Kingdom because they will "never forget" the day the elders made that statement or decision.

Genesis 41 tells of Joseph . . . you know . . . the one who wore the coat that looked like it had been designed by Charley Finley. It was colorful and bright! Joseph had been harshly abused by the events of life. His brothers hated him. They sold him. He was chartered off to Egypt as a slave. In and out of jail, but not guilty, Joseph found life to be what many experience—unfair! Two sons were born to him. "And Joseph named the firstborn Manasseh. 'For,' he said, 'God has made me forget all my trouble and all my father's household'" (v. 51). Forgetting is the key.

How much physical pain we heap upon ourselves because we will not get rid of bad memories. How we torture ourselves with our destructive vows to never let the topic be dropped or the individual forgiven. Joseph did it; with God's help, he forgot.

Then in verse 52, "And he named the second Ephraim, 'For,' he said, 'God has made me fruitful in the land of my affliction.'" Pure gold, friend! Fruitful! When? After he was made to forget!

Fruitful! Where? In the land of affliction! Joseph simply succeeded in the life provided him. The grass was not greener in the next country or in the next year or in the next generation. He found a way to make it produce—bear fruit—in the land of affliction.

This is exactly what makes Jesus so beautifully practical. He does not lead us to find joy by walking twenty feet above the ground. In Him we are transformed. "Therefore, if any man is in Christ, he is a new creature; the old things passed away; behold new things have come" (2 Cor. 5:17). In Christ, in Christ, in Christ! Why? Because He "really" provides the true way to live. Did you catch that? True way to live? What did He say about Himself in John 14:6? "I am the *way,* the *truth,* and the *life*" (italics added). He is the true way to live.

To develop this idea further, consider Romans 8. Verse 35 asks what would cause a person to give up and be separated from the love of Christ. The answer is uniquely simple. "But *in* all these things we overwhelmingly conquer through Him who loved us" (Rom. 8:37—italics added).

You have just discovered one of the secrets of living. We do not gain victory above, around, away from, beyond, or below our difficulties. Because of Jesus, we are winners in life, while so many others are losers. We win in the very middle of the problems. Saturated in alcohol, bewildered by drugs, and racked by worry, humans seek to escape to the better life—but the goal eludes us. Victory is not found in escape; it is found in faith while we are *in* the bind. "For whatever is born of God overcomes the world; and this is the victory that has overcome the world—our faith."

Faith in Jesus—the true way to live—says that even though we find ourselves in circumstances we did not solicit, that very foe is already defeated in Christ! The weapons of doubt dwindle. The practicality of Christ becomes evident. We are able to win *in* the land of affliction; now we can do more than merely exist from day to day. We can really live.

God doesn't lose us; He saves us. God doesn't give us death; He gives us life. Jesus didn't take the healthy and make them ill. He didn't take the whole and make them withered. He healed, loved, gave, and nurtured. Jesus puts real living into routine life!

Can you endure? In Christ you can handle anything! As you consider that He may very well be that real help, think about this: Jesus said, "Come unto Me, all who are weary and heavy-laden, and I will give you rest. Take my yoke upon you, and learn from Me, for I am gentle and humble in heart; and you shall find rest for your souls. For My yoke is easy, and My load is light" (Matt. 11:28–30). So many think that Jesus is a burden—one more attachment in life to make us busier and guiltier. He is quite the opposite.

First, He came to remove sins, not to heap them on us. He makes life easier, not more complex. Consider His statement about the yoke. A yoke allows the ox to pull a load with greater ease. What if there was no yoke? Well, I guess we would have to tie the cart to the ox's tail. Now that could be quite a strain when pulling uphill and very dangerous going downhill. The load could be heavy enough to pull its tail off! The yoke makes it easier to deal with loads.

Let's imagine a situation that calls for some ingenuity. You have a boat and trailer. You have a truck to pull them to the lake. How do you connect the trailer to the truck? You might weld the tongue to the tailgate, but then that wouldn't be very convenient. The only way you could disconnect it would be with a hacksaw or a cutting torch. If you use a chain, the ride would be unsteady and unsafe. What can be done? Well, maybe if a trailer hitch were put on . . . oh, yeah . . . a trailer hitch! How much simpler that would be. That's all Jesus is saying in Matt. 11:28–30. Take His yoke (trailer hitch), for it will make life easier and burdens lighter.

That's what you need, someone to make suggestions as to how you can wade through all those major and minor disasters. Pulling a boat and trailer is a snap with a hitch, but it is a mind-boggling pain without one. Life is easier with Jesus, but it is wearisome without Him. People are always looking for ways to escape from their problems. Alcohol, drugs, crafts, sports, etc., become avenues of distraction. You can soak your mind in alcohol, but sooner or later the difficulty has to be faced. You can avoid the turmoil by going to the lake, but after the fishing is over, you know what's waiting back home, don't you?

Can anyone help? Yes. Jesus encourages us to learn from Him. His meek and lowly attitude make his teaching easy to endure. If He were harsh and bossy, he wouldn't be so inviting. We don't need another source of discouragement. Jesus said He is a source of encouragement and relief.

If you are in Christ and your life still feels like a huge burden, something is wrong. If your Bible class or your ministry or your service to God is a burden, something is involved that didn't come from God. He wants to make life easier, not harder.

This generation needs a breed of Christians that are of joy. Jesus is wonderful. He didn't come to rob us of living. He is no thief (John 10:10)! He wants us to live!

Before we advance to the next phase of this study, do you understand that you cannot escape the "hangnails" of life? Since you must deal with them, do you understand that Jesus is the answer? He is the Way. He is the Truth. He is the Life. He has a plan for life that is more real, more practical than any other. He is a very "down-to-earth" type person. He *literally* came down to earth!

Read the description of Jesus leaving Heaven to come down to earth in Philippians 2, Hebrews 2, and Hebrews 4.

Have this attitude in yourselves which was also in Christ Jesus, who, although He existed in the form of God, did not regard equality with God a thing to be grasped, but emptied Himself, taking the form of a bond-servant, and being made in the likeness of men (Phil. 2:5–7)

He was willing to leave the luxuries of heaven to train on the field of human territory. Jesus is no "classroom savior" who merely learned about humans through a textbook. He became one of us; he walked in our shoes to research the life of these sub-heaven beings—humans. This is an extremely significant factor as we look to Him.

Few realize that Jesus went through aches and pains. That Jesus possibly had mumps or a backache or an upset stomach has never occurred to some. It offends others to insinuate such ordinary symptoms of humanness. Such offense comes because, to many, Jesus isn't real. Not understanding His "earthliness" makes Jesus a "doctrine" for ritualism. Thus He serves no real purpose and ultimately is no real help, because, to many, He just isn't *real*.

When we begin to believe that Jesus experienced cloudy days, humidity, hunger, and fallen arches, then we can believe Him when He says through His Word that He understands. If all He had ever dealt with were cherubim, altars, and seals, then He certainly wouldn't understand what it's like to live in downtown Jerusalem or in upstate New York.

Since then the children share in flesh and blood [are simply human beings], He himself likewise also partook of the same, that through death He might render powerless him who had the power of death, that is, the devil; and might deliver those who through fear of death were subject to slavery all their lives. For assuredly He does not give help to angels, but He gives help to the descendants of Abraham [humans]. Therefore, He had to be *made like his brethren in all things,* that He might become a merciful and faithful high priest [that He might understand what it's like being a person] in things pertaining to God, to make propitiation for the sins of the people. For since He Himself was tempted in that which He has suffered, He is able to come to the aid of those who are tempted (Heb. 2:14–18—italics added).

Skip over to chapter four of Hebrews to find this concept strongly reinforced.

Since then we have a great high priest who passed through the heavens [That He came to earth is the point here.], Jesus, the Son of God, let us hold fast our confession. For we do not have a high priest who cannot sympathize with our weaknesses, but one who has been tempted in all things *as we are,* yet without sin. Let us therefore draw near with confidence to the throne of grace that we may receive mercy and may find grace to help in time of need" (4:14–16—italics added).

When we are in need, we need help. We don't need someone to quote to us the lineup of the 1948

World Series. We need help—now! Life's problems are manageable because the One who is a vital help had "on-the-job training" in the field of human living. Frustration, temptation, irritation—He dealt with it all. So, He now can say to the Father, "Look, I know what it's like down there; it's rough" (1 John 2:1).

Can we make it? "Whatever is born of God overcomes the world; and this is the victory that overcomes the world—our faith" (1 John 5:4).

CHAPTER TWO

Captured by Enemy Pirates
(Wading With Hope)

God is fully aware of our sin problem. "All have sinned and fallen short of the glory of God" (Rom. 3:23). "Therefore, just as through one man sin entered into the world, and death through sin, and so death spread to all men, because all sinned" (Rom. 5:12). "But God demonstrates His own love toward us, in that while we were yet sinners, Christ died for us" (Rom. 5:8). God continually reveals that He knows we are in a sin-bind.

The reason Jesus is such good news is that He provides our release from captivity. Sinners are held hostage by the sin dilemma. We must get rid of this despicable problem. But how? Who will help? You guessed it . . . Jesus helps (Heb. 4:16). ". . . having now been justified by His blood, we shall be saved from the wrath of God through Him. For while we were enemies, we were reconciled to God through the death of His Son, much more, having been reconciled we shall be saved by His life" (Rom. 5:9–10).

Jesus didn't half-heartedly die for us. He voluntarily surrendered, becoming obedient to the point of death, even death on a cross. What if He had been killed in a three-camel crash? His life would have been taken, not given. "The Son of Man came to give His life a ransom for many" (Matt. 20:28). We were the hostages. He didn't simply pay the ransom. *He is the ransom!* Jesus died that we might live. He didn't contribute a pint of blood at the office as an expression of a community-spirited fellow. He shed His blood that we could escape the sin/hostage crisis! "In Him we have redemption through His blood, the forgiveness of our trespasses according to the riches of His grace, which He lavished upon us." (Eph. 1:7–8).

As in everything else God does, He has provided a certain way of escape. Do we fear that Jesus may have done an excellent job of dying but will do a questionable job of saving? Are we afraid He won't be able to save us from our sins? Not only must we have a generation who believes in Him as the Son, we must believe He is capable and abundantly able as a Savior.

At this time I introduce to you a thrilling New Testament concept that is often overlooked—largely because we don't know how to pronounce the word. The word is "propitiation." Furthermore, it is the very core of the good news. Propitiation expresses strongly that the blood of Christ pacifies God's anger. Consider His wrath:

> For the wrath of God is revealed from heaven against all ungodliness and unrighteousness

of men who suppress the truth in unrighteousness (Rom. 1:18).

But to those who are selfishly ambitious and do not obey the truth, but obey unrighteousness, wrath and indignation. There will be tribulation and distress for every soul of man who does evil, of the Jew first and also of the Greek (Rom. 2:8–9).

For after all it is only just for God to repay with affliction those who afflict you, and to give relief to you who are afflicted and to us as well when the Lord Jesus shall be revealed from heaven with his mighty angels in flaming fire, dealing out retribution to those who do not know God and to those who do not obey the gospel of our Lord Jesus. And these will pay the penalty of eternal destruction, away from the presence of the Lord and from the glory of His power (2 Thess. 1:7–9).

What is mankind to do? The worst holocaust of all time will be experienced if a way of escape is not provided. There is a way and this is why the gospel literally means "good news." The remedy is propitiation. Watch the declaration of deliverance beautifully unfold right before your very eyes.

Sinners who believe in Jesus will be . . .

justified as a gift by His grace through the redemption which is in Christ Jesus; whom God displayed publicly as a *propitiation* in

His blood through faith. This was to demonstrate His righteousness, because in the forbearance of God He passed over the sins previously committed; for the demonstration, I say, of His righteousness at the present time, that He might be just and the justifier of the one who has faith in Jesus (Rom. 3:25–26—italics added).

Keep in mind that propitiation pacifies the anger of God. The blood of Jesus cleanses our sins!

Therefore, He had to be made like His brethren [that is, like you and me: human] in all things, that He might become a merciful and faithful high priest in things pertaining to God, to make propitiation for the sins of the people. For since He Himself was tempted in that which He has suffered, He is able to *come to the aid* of those who are tempted (Heb. 2:17–18—italics added).

God says to Jesus from His throne in heaven, "Son, why do those people behave that way? Why do they think like that?" And Jesus replies, "Father, I know they do wrong, but it is different being human. A human sometimes does what he knows he shouldn't. Then the next thing you know, he will turn right around and not do something he knows he should" (Rom. 7:14–24). The blood Jesus shed dissolves God's anger.

"My little children, I am writing these things to you that you may not sin" (1 John 2:1).

"What's that, John?"

"I said, 'Don't be sinning!' " "And if anyone sins, we have an advocate with the Father, Jesus Christ the righteous."

Allow me to insert a comforting word here. We are told not to sin. But our problem is that we will sin. "If we say we have no sin, we are deceiving ourselves, and the truth is not in us" (1 John 1:8). When we keep from sinning we are safe. But as we sin, is there any security to be found? 1 John 2:1 insists that Jesus will stand alongside us as our personal attorney. God watches us. He sees that we sin and He brings us to the judge. As we approach the bench, Jesus arises with these words. "Your Honor, if it pleases the court, I know Terry personally. He confessed me before men. Your Honor, there is sin in his life. I have his file and chose to represent his case. I volunteer to be his lawyer."

I'm here to tell you, we sinners have help. Notice what the Scripture says, "And if anyone sins, we have an advocate." Jesus arises to help when we sin. We have the concept that He will only be good to us if we don't sin. And that is discouraging, because we do sin. If our Saviour can only help us when we are good, why do we need a saviour? A "saviour" is like a lifeguard who comes to the rescue of someone who is drowning.

Please be assured that I am not leading you to a false security. The Word teaches that the blood works better on our sins than Pinetop does on sink stains. His blood wasn't shed because we were good, but because we were ungodly (Rom. 5:6). The blood doesn't aid us if we have no sin. It works only when there is sin. "But if we walk in the light as He Himself is in the light, we have fellowship with one another, and the blood of Jesus His Son cleanses us from all sin" (1 John 1:7).

End of insert, now back to *propitiation*. We are still dealing with 1 John 2:1. Listen as verse 2 explains, "And He Himself is the propitiation for our sins; and not for ours only, but also for those of the whole world." Surely you can see why I say that propitiation is at the very heart of the gospel. It is terrifically good news!

Consider one more text.

> By this the love of God was manifested in us, that God has sent His only begotten Son into the world so that we might live through Him. In this is love, not that we loved God, but that He loved us and sent His Son to be the propitiation for our sins (1 John 4:9–10).

This message is God-given. If Jesus can't save us from our sins, He might just as well have been a quarterback, an accountant, or a lumberjack. If His blood doesn't cleanse sins, He wasted His time on the cross because we have a sin problem, and we need help! But from the above Scriptures it is crystal clear that He does function with saving power.

Once again, read with joy the beauty of the following statement.

> But God demonstrates His own love toward us, in that while we were yet sinners, Christ died for us. Much more then, having now been

justified by his blood, we shall be saved from the wrath of God through Him (Rom. 5:8–9).

When we surrender our life to Jesus, we find that we have much help.

For we do not have a high priest who cannot sympathize with our weaknesses, but one who has been tempted in all things as we are, yet without sin. Let us [sinners] therefore draw near with confidence to the throne of grace, that we may receive mercy and may find grace to help in time of need (Heb. 4:15, 16).

This chapter is the best news I know of in all the world and its history. Aren't you thankful to God you heard such good news? Don't you think others would also be thankful and enthused? Share this message with others soon!

CHAPTER THREE

No Longer Driven by Winds and Waves
(Wading With Maturity)

Have you ever noticed how temporary the commitment of some is to God? Enthusiasm is high immediately following the new birth. For some, though, such vigor evaporates. There is a reason for this, as you will discover in the reading of Matthew 13:18–23.

Hear then the parable of the sower. When anyone hears the word of the Kingdom, and does not understand it, the evil one comes and snatches away what has been sown in his heart. This is the one on whom seed was sown beside the road. And the one on whom the seed was sown on the rocky places, this is the man who hears the word, and immediately receives it with joy; yet he has *no firm root* in himself, but is only *temporary,* and when affliction or persecution arises because of the word, immediately he falls away.

And the one on whom seed was sown among the thorns, this is the man who hears the word, and the worry of the world, and the deceitfulness of riches choke the word, and it becomes unfruitful. And the one on whom seed was sown on the good ground, this is the man who hears the word and understands it; who indeed bears fruit, and brings forth some a hundredfold, some sixty, and some thirty (italics added).

The Alpha and the Omega (the beginning and the end) of evangelism and fruitbearing are precisely explained in that parable. The goal of this book is to help people understand the Word. It is not enough to simply scatter the Word. We must prepare the soil so the seed can be received. The first one to hear the Word in the parable simply did not understand.

Religious "junk food" is everywhere. On the air, in magazines, books, tracts, and even in sermons. Those of us who devote our lives to communicating His revelation must consider the hearer, as well as the source. We must realize that we must till the field before we sow the seed. Sometimes the land needs to be cleared of its stumps before it is able to receive the seed, much less bear a crop.

Let us now concentrate on the person in the parable to whom this chapter is directed: the temporary Christian. How sad to find a heart so ready for the good news, only to see that person fall away. It is my conviction that we can help such people to be fruitful instead of being casualties.

What causes a person to be temporary? The

No Longer Driven by Winds and Waves

Scripture indicates it is because they have no firm root. Therefore, when affliction and stress arise, that individual's heart becomes discouraged.

So simple! Why does anyone quit serving the King? Always because some parasite of discouragement saps his drive, and he bows to the pressure. To adequately reach a solution, let us pursue the problem a bit further.

Peter found himself in one of the most privileged positions of all history. Men have walked along the most beautiful of sites. Men have walked on the moon. But no man, except Peter, ever walked on water with Jesus. Although it was a brief trek, he accomplished what no one else did. Why did he eventually begin to sink? Because he saw the wind!

Now, let's go to work on this. Peter was on the right course. Yet, he was distracted: discouraged from doing what he intended. He bowed to the prevailing distress of the winds. He took his eyes off Jesus. If we are to help another, we must guide them to be rooted in Jesus. Their faith must not be expected. It must be developed! If we expect a garden to survive, we must continually protect it from weeds. How can we do any less with souls?

James 1:6–8 warns us to be careful how we wade on the waters of life. "But let him ask in faith without any doubting, for the one who doubts is like the surf of the sea driven and tossed by the wind. For let not that man expect that he will receive anything from the Lord, being a double-minded man, unstable in all his ways."

How do we help? One way is to encourage one

another to serve only the Master. "No man can serve two masters," said Jesus in Matt. 6:24. Single-minded followers of the Christ are the ones who effectively wade through life. Intentional servanthood develops mustard-seed faith. We must help each other to take action. When He speaks, we must respond.

Listen as Jesus describes those who will successfully wade, who will endure the driving winds and waves like those Peter may have seen.

> Therefore everyone who hears these words of Mine, and acts upon them, may be compared to a wise man, who built his house upon the rock. And the rain descended, and the floods came, and the winds blew, and burst against that house; and yet it did not fall, for it had been founded upon the rock.
>
> And everyone who hears these words of Mine, and does not act upon them, will be like a foolish man, who built his house upon the sand. And the floods came and the winds blew, and burst against that house; and it fell, and great was its fall (Matt. 7:24–27).

We wade through life in one of two classes—wise or foolish. Not only must we be guided to serve only one master, *the* Master, we must help others properly build. That's how we can affect the "stick around/fall away ratio." Faith is more solidly founded when guidance is given for sturdy building.

How can this be done? With reference to equipping (developing), growing, building, and faith, note God's comments in Eph. 4:12–16. Gifts of various ministries had been presented . . .

> for the equipping of the saints for the work of service, to the building up of the body of Christ; until we all attain to the unity of the faith, and of the knowledge of the Son of God, to a mature man, to the measure of the stature which belongs to the fullness of Christ.
>
> As a result, we are no longer to be children tossed here and there by waves, and carried about by every wind of doctrine, by the trickery of men, by craftiness in deceitful scheming; but speaking the truth in love, we are to grow up in all aspects into Him, who is the head, even Christ, from whom the whole body, being fitted and held together by that which every joint supplies, according to the proper working of each individual part, causes the growth of the body for the building up of itself in love.

How do we develop that root in others so that they can endure the winds and waves while wading? It is accomplished by training individuals for service and instilling in them the characteristics of Christ. These characteristics are called maturity. The mature man, James says, is the one no longer tossed about by winds and waves. The storms may hit, but the root keeps the mature one from falling or breaking.

There is a tremendous need for creative and renewed thinking as to how we may do a better job of equipping. From the beginning of this study, it has been biblically verified that the person without a firm root will fold under pressure and distress. Christ must be presented only as real and as practical as He is.

He is, however, more personally experiential than we sometimes confess. Knowing Christ is more than an academic agreement that He is God's Son. Knowing Him involves trusting, sensing, walking, and living in Him. He is not a vague "maybe" that serves as a nice topic for a Bible class. God, when put to the test, described the reality of His existence when he declared "I AM!"

We must, must, must, bring people to genuinely and practically know the personality of Jesus ". . . so that Christ may dwell in your hearts through faith; and that you, being rooted [there it is] and grounded in love, may be able to comprehend with all the saints what is the breadth and length and height and depth, and to know the love of Christ which surpasses knowledge, that you may be filled up to all the fullness of God" (Eph. 3:17–19).

Let me ask you this. As stated, how does one come to "know that which surpasses knowledge"? I believe it's by experience. I couldn't explain to you how a refrigerator works if my life depended on it. But surpassing the knowledge of how it works, I experientially know how to benefit from a refrigerator. Any atheist knows that a refrigerator refrigerates. Why can't they understand that a Savior saves? Because, they want to approach Him from statistics, measurements, and human wisdom. Knowing Christ and His love cannot be described on a 3 × 5 card and filed in a shoe box. The love of Christ is touched, felt, sensed, revealed, and lived due to one thing . . . *faith*.

How do we wade through winds and waves that create distress and danger? To sum up what has been said in this chapter, we need to *keep our eyes on Jesus*. Study Him. He told us to come learn of Him. He also said, "And this is eternal life, that they may know Thee, the only true God, and Jesus Christ whom Thou hast sent" (John 17:3).

Eternal life is knowing the Father and the Son. A secretary can handle mail for years for a corporation. She can correspond with clients and customers regularly and yet never know them. What are they like? How do they feel? What are their goals? She doesn't know. To her, they are merely a signature beneath a company letterhead, maybe a number to be invoiced. Personally? She wouldn't know them from Roger Wornout.

Christians cannot be so vaguely unfamiliar with Jesus and survive. He must be more than a name in a songbook and a word at the close of a prayer. He is our life! He is our energy! He is to be known.

Therefore, we must diligently study Him. Learning of Him is learning the way, the truth, and the life . . . the eternal Life! His characteristics and personality need to be molding ours. When Christ dwells in our hearts through faith, and when we are rooted and grounded in love, this leads us to be filled with the fullness of God (Eph. 3:17–19).

Filled with God, indwelt by Christ, and all the while being rooted, we will no longer be driven by winds and waves.

CHAPTER FOUR

Handling the Insalts of Life
(Wading With Mercy)

Of course the title of this chapter is a slight play on words—combining insults with the stinging salt of the ocean's waves. And we all have abundant opportunities to deal with "insalts." We are constantly challenged by domineering personalities, overbearing circumstances, and unfortunate mishaps. To some extent everyone wades through them.

Sharp confrontations with life should not surprise us. What is of supreme importance is how we handle them. The way to be victorious over challenges is the Master's way. He walked our walk. To us, the Hebrew writer said,

> Therefore, since we have so great a cloud of witnesses surrounding us, let us also lay aside every encumbrance, and the sin which so easily entangles us, and let us run with endurance the race that is set before us, fixing our eyes on Jesus, the author and perfecter of faith, who for the joy set before Him endured the cross, despising the shame, and has set down

at the right hand of the throne of God. For consider Him who has endured such hostility by sinners against Himself, so that you may not grow weary and lose heart (Heb. 12: 1–3).

Very clearly, we are directed to follow in His steps. Jesus didn't enjoy the cross, but He did enjoy the life to follow. He looked beyond the suffering and the insults. Never was His vision blurred by sarcastic remarks or discouraging situations. We can succeed as He did.

Much of our distress is brought on by our inability to genuinely forgive and forget. As Jesus hung on the cross, approaching death, He asked the Father to forgive the murderers (His murderers). Now we can understand why God asks us to fix our eyes on Him: the perfecter of faith.

One characteristic that enables us to wade alongside insults is what I call the mercy factor. Mercy is cheapened when viewed only as an academic word. We can discuss and re-discuss its meaning from a glossary, but when faced with real trials, it is of little help for someone to hand us a dictionary. We need mercy in action.

How does mercy behave? If mercy wore clothes, ate food, enjoyed recreation, and leaned toward pure religion, how would it appear?

It would be as God is. "But love your enemies, and do good, and lend, expecting nothing in return; and your reward will be great, and you will be sons of the Most High; for He Himself is kind to ungrateful and evil men. Be merciful, just as your Father is merciful" (Luke 6:35–36).

At times, it is hard to love our friends, let alone our enemies. It can be quite a grimacing experience to loan money or mowers or machines, but to expect nothing in return . . . I'm pressed by this one. I don't mind helping when my assistance is appreciated, but help the ungrateful bum, forget it! I'm nobody's fool!

Mercy shifts all of that. We are no longer insalted. We are compassionate toward others. God, at the cross, had to choose between the life of His enemies or the life of His Son. He let His Son's blood be shed. He spared the enemy. Be merciful, just as your Father is merciful. How different this world would be if each of us could let mercy wade wearing our clothes, our minds, and our actions.

The startling element in all of this is that such compassion isn't to be shown only to those who ignorantly or accidentally insalt you. It is to be demonstrated even to those who purposefully, intentionally hurt you. Human beings decidedly nailed Jesus to the tree, for the precise purpose of bringing about His death. If He had asked that they be forgiven for something out of their control, that would be one thing. But to pursue their forgiveness during their intentional vandalism to His flesh is quite convincing that mercy comes from the nature of heaven, and not from earth. We don't naturally think that way.

This is such an extreme. Does God really expect this kind of mercy from us? Keep in mind that Jesus taught it and handled Himself accordingly. Stephen thought he meant it.

Acts chapter seven tells us that Stephen had just been chosen to serve in a special capacity. His preaching upset the hearers to the point that a riot broke out. Verses 54–60 describe the final moments of his life. The mob despised his words. They drove him from the city limits and began stoning him. Here's the question: In this setting, how far does God's child need to carry this "mercy thing"?

Stephen carried it as far as our Master taught him. "And falling on his knees, he cried out with a loud voice, 'Lord, do not hold this sin against them!' And having said this, he fell asleep." Would that have been your last request? Or, would it have been more like, "God get 'em and get 'em good!"?

Now read Romans 12:19–21. (Is God serious about this? Listen.) "Never [When, God? Never!] take your own revenge, beloved, but leave room for the wrath of God." By the time we get done with others, there isn't any room left for God's wrath. We wrath them to death all by ourselves. "For it is written, 'Vengeance is mine, I will repay,' says the Lord." What do we do, then, with those who trespass on our wading pools? " 'But if your enemy is hungry, feed him, and if he is thirsty, give him a drink; for in so doing you will heap burning coals upon his head.' Do not be overcome by evil, but overcome evil with good."

How do we wade through life with insalters standing at every intersection? He's telling us. Having studied Romans 12:19–21, read the preceding nine verses. Notice how verses 10–18 are worded as if every phrase was to guide us through such trials.

> Be devoted to one another in brotherly love; give preference to one another in honor; not lagging behind in diligence, fervent in spirit, serving the Lord; rejoicing in hope, persevering in tribulation, devoted to prayer, contributing to the needs of the saints, practicing hospitality. Bless those who persecute you; bless and curse not. Rejoice with those who rejoice, and weep with those who weep.
> Be of the same mind toward one another; do not be haughty in mind, but associate with the lowly. Do not be wise in your own estimation. Never pay back evil for evil to anyone. Respect what is right in the sight of all men. If possible, so far as it depends on you, be at peace with all men. Never take your own revenge.

What daring advice! What a neighborhood we would have if only a few would practice this! And this is to be exampled by God's children. This is how we handle the insalts of life.

"The straw that broke the camel's back" communicates that no more misuse or abuse will be tolerated. However, to be controlled by the love of Christ (2 Cor. 5:14) necessitates that camel's backs no longer be broken. Love is not provoked and does not take into account a wrong suffered (1 Cor. 13:5). No matter how many wrongs pile up, we are not to issue the ultimatum—"that does it!"

But aren't we taking this to an extreme God never intended? After all, even the biggest of hearts can only be expected to handle so much. After so many incidents, intentional or not, one finally has to draw the line and say, "That's it!" How much does God expect us to forgive?

"Lord, how often shall my brother sin against me and I forgive him? Up to seven times?" Jesus said to him, "I do not say to you, up to seven times, but up to seventy times seven" (Matt. 18:21–22).

"For this reason," He continues in verse 23, "the kingdom of heaven may be compared to a certain king who wished to settle accounts with his slaves. . . ." Whatever is found in the rest of that story will be the revelation from God as to how we ought to handle the insults dealt one to another. We will find just how compassionate, forgiving, and merciful God expects us to be. Read the account in verses 24–35.

In settling the accounts, a slave was brought before the king who owed thousands and thousands of dollars. The servant said he didn't have a dime to pay back. The master felt compassion for his hopeless dilemma and forgave him the debt. In turn, that forgiven slave went out to a co-slave and demanded the meager dollar which was owed. The co-slave had no means to repay. The forgiven slave began to choke the co-slave (probably trying to get him to cough up the money!). The poor slave was cast into prison because he didn't pay back the dollar.

When the king heard what the forgiven slave had done he said, "You wicked slave. I forgave you all that debt because you entreated me. Should you not also have had mercy on your fellow slave, even as I had mercy on you?"

Why? Each of us, as we contact the blood of Christ, has many accounts settled. Jesus paid our debt. It was a huge bill. There was no way we could repay it. We are forgiven the sin of wrong actions, all of them! We are forgiven the sin of wrong thoughts, all of them! We are forgiven every sin, every potential condemner. We are forgiven all.

When others sin against us, God watches our temptation to be impatient. When we are just about ready to collect our "pound of flesh," He reminds us of the king and the slave. What has another person done against you that is anywhere near what you have done against God? Compared to my debt that God "wrote off" because of the blood payment, the "write off" we issue toward those who insalt us isn't equal to a dollar's worth.

A Christian is forgiven so much, abundantly forgiven. We are to be merciful in return—seventy times seven! That's pretty extreme. And now you know the rest of the story!

Mercy isn't only forgiving, it is also giving. A certain man was beaten and left for dead in a ditch (Luke 10:30–37). A priest saw the hurting man, but he passed by. Another religious official did the same. Then a lowly fellow saw the victim, bandaged him, took him to a motel, and stayed with him overnight. He told the man at the desk he would pay whatever bill this stranger ran up.

" 'Which of these three do you think proved to be a neighbor to the man who fell into the robbers' hands?" And he said, 'The one who showed mercy toward him.' And Jesus said to him, 'Go and do the same.' "

This next statement may be a little strong, but it needs your most sober attention. An individual will go to hell in the fast lane if he is not merciful. Extreme? Hardly. I consider this next verse to be one of the most serious and weighty of all Scripture. "So speak and so act as those who are to be judged by the law of liberty. For judgment will be merciless to the one who has shown no mercy; mercy triumphs over judgment" (James 2:12–13).

To the one who helps the helpless and forgives the stone-throwing, tongue-wagging enemy, mercy will conquer in the day of judgment. To the one who deals grudge for grudge, hate for hate, and stubbornness for stubbornness, conviction and sentencing will be his eternal lot. Now it makes much sense when Jesus said, in Matt. 5:7, "Blessed are the merciful [Why is that such a big deal?], for they shall receive mercy."

> For what credit is there if, when you sin and are harshly treated, you endure it with patience? But if when you do what is right and suffer for it you patiently endure it, this finds favor with God (1 Pet. 2:20).

When Jesus was reviled, He didn't revile in return. While suffering, He didn't threaten. He entrusted Himself to Him who judges righteously. As a result He bore our sins in His body on the cross (1 Pet. 2:23–24). We are to take up our cross and follow Him (Luke 9:23).

Taking up the cross is not merely a spiritualized act. It sets our lives in proper position. We find ourselves deep in suffering just as Jesus did. No threats, no tantrums—just a forbearing spirit that compassionately cares for the enemy.

The position is so important. When positioned on our self-made throne, we return insults. Properly fashioned on our cross, we bear up under the strain with mercy—the same kind of mercy we expect from the Father.

"But if you had known what this means, 'I desire compassion, and not a sacrifice,' you would not have condemned the innocent." How do we handle the insults of life? Show the opponent, who causes you tremendous suffering, the love and the mercy of one who is positioned on the cross. There will always be enemies daring you to come down off the cross, just as they dared Jesus. But you do as He did. Stay until death.

Again, fix your eyes on Jesus who endured the cross, despising the shame, for the joy that would come later. You will be much more stable in your wade through life, if you can begin to love the hateful. Since He walked on water, we can wade through life.

CHAPTER FIVE

I'm Going in Over My Head
(Wading Through Suffering)

Some Christians feel that if life isn't a bed of roses, God must be against them. When things go wrong, they think this is a signal that God is displeased. This chapter is aimed at those who feel they are about to go under in their walk with Christ.

First, refer to the Word in 1 Peter 2:18–25. The context is one of suffering, with emphasis—strong emphasis—on submission during such suffering. Verse 18 calls for submission, even to the unreasonable. Verse 19 encourages us that we find favor with God when we suffer unjustly. Verse 20 continues by saying that when you suffer for doing what is right, and endure, it pleases God. Now, verse 21 is very, very significant in that it shows we are called to suffer. "For you have been called for this purpose, since Christ also suffered for you, leaving you an example for you to follow in His steps."

The life of Jesus was one of suffering. Isaiah 53 portrays Him as the "Suffering Servant." "And being found in appearance as a man, He humbled Himself by becoming obedient to the point of death, even death on a cross" (Phil. 2:8).

We are called to suffer. If no one tells us this ahead of time, we may panic when difficulty hits. "For to you it has been granted for Christ's sake, not only to believe in Him but also to suffer for His sake, experiencing the same conflict which you saw in me and now hear to be in me" (Phil. 1:29–30).

The road to the cross is jammed with critics. The path of discipleship is likewise snared. For the person who desires to make Jesus merely an ornament for a nice holiday weekend, there will be no suffering in the road. And for the one who chooses to make Him a weekend social club president, suffering won't be on the agenda. However, for the believer, the serious disciple, suffering will be at the center of serving.

Jesus was beaten, spat upon, mocked, and finally suffered capital punishment. Stephen was stoned to death (Acts 7). Paul was imprisoned, beaten times without number, often in danger of death. He was in danger from rivers, robbers, countrymen, Gentiles, and secret-agent disciples. He went without sleep, food, and shelter (2 Cor. 11:23–28).

When you look at your problems, don't lose heart, and don't let them intimidate you or hinder your service. Always remember the purpose for which you were called—to suffer (1 Peter 2:21).

This concept is brought forth in Rom. 8:28–39. Verse 28 is always quoted when something goes wrong. If someone wins a million dollars, no one says, "Well, just remember that everything works together for good." That verse is used only when suffering is being processed. Notice for whom good things work . . . those who love God and those who are called according to his purpose. What is the purpose? The same as Jesus' . . . to suffer as a servant! That's why Paul wrote in verse 31, "If God is for us, who is against us?" When you feel that you are going under, that God has forgotten you, don't forget that suffering is normal for the disciple.

Who shall separate us from the love of Christ? What will finally cause you to go under as you wade through life: too much push from the preacher, too much pressure from committees, some decision by the leaders, neglect by others? Illness? Business? Sports? Vacations? Can any of these separate us from the love of Christ? Shall tribulation, worry, pressure, hunger, nothing to wear, peril, or war? In every one of these problems, Paul says, we win (v. 37). Not an enemy do we face that has not already been whipped and put in its place by Jesus.

How does the follower keep from sinking with worry over unemployment, divorce, death, malicious rumors, etc.? By remaining with God and being determined that nothing will ever separate the two of you.

> For I am convinced that neither death, nor life, nor angels, nor principalities, nor things present, nor things to come, nor powers, nor

height, nor depth, nor any other created thing, shall be able to separate us from the love of God, which is in Christ Jesus our Lord (Rom. 8:38–39).

Therefore we do not lose heart, but though our outer man is decaying, yet our inner man is being renewed day by day. For momentary, light affliction is producing for us an eternal weight of glory far beyond all comparison, while we look not at the things which are seen, but at the things which are not seen; for the things which are seen are temporal, but the things which are not seen are eternal (2 Cor. 4:16–18).

One way to keep from going under is to concentrate on the eternal—the invisible, the unseen. Consider how foolish the visible is. Americans habitually complain about two problems. One, we don't have enough money, and two, we weigh too much. The solution is obvious. Don't spend your money on food! But that's too easy. We'd rather be broke and bulky. That way we can worry more.

Thus it is with all the visible (what we tend to call the real): it is so temporary and yet demands our fullest attention.

On the other hand, the believer will give heed to the invisible. He will not give up his wading trek, because his eyes are fixed on the eternal. Our suffering is no longer a curse, but a blessing. When we approach the deeper level, where we could possibly go under, God is given the opportunity to do His stuff.

Have you ever noticed how God shines in the most gloomy, hopeless situations? Abraham and Sarah were too old. Noah didn't know what it was like to come in out of the rain. Joseph was in the pits. Moses was upstream without a paddle. Gideon's outnumbered troops fought off Midian with pitchers, torches, and a bunch of old bugles bought at a garage sale! The children of Israel would have been up to their eyebrows in fish had the Jordan river not parted.

Throughout the Bible, we find individuals and groups facing the feasibility that they may go under. Everyone who succeeded, kept their eyes on the eternal. They were not distracted by the temporal. And so it is with you and me.

Must we suffer? Or, am I an extremist, unnecessarily disturbing the common practice of being just an ordinary, likeable, no-source-of-trouble worshipper? The New Testament is riddled with the truth of suffering. We have looked at several examples. Time does not permit me to elaborate on all of these. Read and study Matt. 10:32–39; John 15:19–21, 16:33; 2 Cor. 7:4; Heb. 11:25,37,38 and Rev. 7:14. Once you have covered those, read Matt. 12:14 and proceed to Acts 9:16, 14:22, 20:23; Rom. 8:36; Phil. 3:10, 1 Thess. 3:3–4, and then observe: "And indeed, all who desire to live godly in Christ Jesus will be persecuted" (2 Tim. 3:12).

There may always be those within God's ranks who deny that Christians will be persecuted. They will always feel, as Peter did in Matthew 16 when Jesus said He must suffer, that it just isn't *that* necessary. Dear reader, it is, it is, it is!

The truth will not stop telling us that suffering is a must. How did Jesus conclude the beatitudes? He said, blessed are those who suffer unjustly (Matt. 5:10–12). How does the servant wade through unfair life? By going beyond the expected, by suffering the second mile (Matt. 5:38–48).

Jesus told His disciples that He must suffer (Matt. 16:21). Peter didn't buy it for a minute. "God forbid it, Lord! This shall never happen to you" (Matt. 16:22). Then Jesus turned to Peter, told him he was a problem, and that he had his mind on man's interests, not God's. When following man's interests, we will always try to avoid punishment. But God needs us to suffer.

Why do we need to experience discomfort? Three reasons, at least, for being afflicted are found in 2 Cor. 1:3–11. First, if we have been afflicted, we are able to comfort another who suffers (v. 4). Our ability to help someone in distress is much greater if we have experienced the same trauma. Jesus knows what it is like to walk in our shoes. Therefore, He is able to come to our aid (Heb. 2:18). Paul experienced many distressing moments. Therefore we find comfort in his God and his writings. When we allow ourselves the privilege of hurting, we then find ability to aid others when they ache.

Secondly, we are afflicted for others salvation (v. 6). When the church willingly, aggressively shines as Christ, it will suffer. And, when it willingly, aggressively suffers, others will be saved. Show me the church member who will not allow himself to be embarrassed, ridiculed, or perplexed, and I'll show you the member who doesn't do any soul winning. Find a newly converted Christian, and nearby you'll find his teacher—one who risked rejection so that another might obey.

Consider Jesus in this regard. "Although He was a Son, He learned obedience *from the things which he suffered.* And having been made perfect, he became to all those who obey Him the source of eternal salvation" (Heb. 5:8–9—italics added).

There it is, even in the life of Jesus! He is the source of salvation because He suffered. What if He had refused to be afflicted? What if He had walked away from the responsibility of the cross? If such had been the case, no one could be saved. So it is with us. If we will suffer, we will lead others to Jesus. If we excuse ourselves, we will never lead one to Him.

Finally, 2 Cor. 1:9 delivers a third reason that we endure. "Indeed, we had the sentence of death within ourselves in order that we should not trust in ourselves, but in God who raises the dead." Agonizing Christians are characterized by a dependence on God. Their source of energy is not self. It is God. The apostle Paul was in misery because of a thorn in the flesh (2 Cor. 12:7–10). Listen to him explain it.

> And because of the surpassing greatness of the revelations, for this reason, *to keep me*

from exalting myself, there was given me a thorn in the flesh, a messenger of Satan to buffet me—to keep me from exalting myself!

Concerning this I entreated the Lord three times that it might depart from me. And He has said to me, "My grace is sufficient for you, for power is perfected in weakness." Most gladly, therefore, I will rather boast about my weaknesses, that the power of Christ may dwell in me. Therefore I am well content with weaknesses, with insults, with distresses, with persecutions, with difficulties, for Christ's sake; *for when I am weak, then I am strong* (italics added).

And there we have it. Our infirmities serve as opportunities for God to demonstrate His power. When you are about to go under, thank God for it. Be of the attitude of Paul—boast about your inferiorities, imperfections, and problems. He said in Phil. 3:8–11 that he gladly suffered the loss of everything for the privilege of knowing Jesus. Are you about to go under? Consider this whole chapter as the "under" statement of life!

CHAPTER SIX

Buried at Sea
(Wading in Obedience)

It is a tremendous blessing to be saved. Whether it dawns on us very much, it is a tremendous thing to be saved. Of all the major catastrophies in the past, or even during our lifetime, that billions hear no good news is the most catastrophic! Satan is awesomely powerful; and he tricks and betrays and deceives and blinds people to keep them from entering the kingdom of God. As we study the Word of God, it sobers us to realize the impact Satan has on the human race. There are still nations that have not been reached by the Word of God. Even worse—there are nations that have the Word of God, but are being blinded by Satan.

We are most fortunate if we come to know the truth as taught in the Scriptures. Many view religion as a smorgasboard where you pick and choose what you want to believe. Anything from meditation to receiving Jesus in your heart is taught as a way to salvation. Satan says, "Be religious, just as long as you don't believe what the Son of God taught."

In Acts 2:37, the Scripture says: "Now when

they heard this they were pierced to the heart and said to Peter and to the apostles, 'Brethren what shall we do?'" Acts 2:38 bombards us with eternal impact. Satan bombards the world with all kinds of concepts that say everything except what the Scripture says. In spite of the conflicting messages, I am convinced that many sincerely ask one question: "What do I need to do to get to Heaven?"

In Acts 22:10 the question is asked, "What shall I do, Lord?" This shows that people really want to know. In Acts 16:30 we read, "What shall I do to be saved?" When this question is asked today, radio beams project throughout our nation saying this and that and little matches up.

Jesus taught in John 3:16 that God so loved the world that whoever would believe in Him wouldn't perish but would have everlasting life. Acts 10:43 says, "Of Him all the prophets bear witness that through His name everyone who believes in Him receives forgiveness for sins." Many respond, "God so loved the world that He gave his son. I believe, therefore, I have my sins forgiven and I'm going to Heaven." But, that isn't all God said.

Open your Bibles to Rom. 10:13 and I'll confuse you some more. "Whoever will call upon the name of the Lord will be saved." That says it in black and white: Whoever will call upon the name of the Lord will be saved. So religious groups start saying that all you need to do is call upon the name of the Lord. So you call upon the name of the Lord . . . that's good! Continue on, though.

Verse 9: "If you confess with your mouth Jesus

is Lord and believe in your heart that God raised Him from the dead you shall be saved." Now, does that say that if you confess *and* believe you will be saved? It says it! Look in verse 10. "For with the heart man believes resulting in righteousness and with the mouth he confesses resulting in salvation." I know that earlier we read that when you believe you are saved. Does Scripture contradict itself? No.

Sometimes I get to thinking that I am a little too dogmatic about this thing. My emotions so yearn for people to be saved that—friend—I would just as soon God would have said that all we must do is believe. Better yet, I would rather that God said everybody is saved. But the fact is God just didn't say that. We must untangle all the airwaves and literature that contradict God's teaching on salvation. *In verse 10,* We can see that several things are involved in being saved.

Someone says, "I'm just going to call upon the name of the Lord." That's tremendous. It ought to be done.

"And, I'm going to believe." That's tremendous. It ought to be done.

"And I'm going to confess Jesus with my mouth." Great!

"But I don't have to be baptized, do I?"

Listen to this. In Acts 22:16 an amazing statement is made. "And now why do you delay, arise and be baptized and wash away your sins calling on His name." How do you call on His name? You do it in a process that begins when you believe that He is the son of God. Scripture says that belief results in righteousness. And, when you confess with your mouth—salvation is the result. You need to call on His name to be saved. And, Acts 22:16 says that when you arise to have your sins washed away, then you have called on His name.

In John 8:24, the Scripture says that "unless you believe that I am He you shall die in your sins." Now the logical thing to think is to reverse that and say: I believe that He is, so I will not die in my sins. Most radio evangelism and literature teaches that if you receive Jesus in your heart, you will be saved. But the Bible doesn't teach it that way.

The tragedy is that the teaching is so clear and simple. No one who argues against baptism would say that all you need to do is call upon the name of the Lord, that you don't have to believe in Him if you don't want to. Nobody would say that. But they will say it is all right to simply believe in Him and that you don't have to be baptized if you don't want to.

I have heard the following hypothetical question several times: What if a guy was walking down the aisle and he died before he was ever baptized? Would he be lost? As an answer, I would say: What if Jesus died on the way to the cross and never made it, would we be saved? The answer is no. We wouldn't be saved. Jesus had to go to the cross to die for our sins. His blood had to be shed. Our salvation is in His blood. We must contact the blood. And the point is, He did! The other point is, we can obey.

If someone dies while walking down the aisle

to be baptized, God will make the decision about his soul. But, I haven't noticed any dying at that moment. So, we don't need to make imaginary moments.

Luke 13:3 says that unless you repent you shall all likewise perish. So we see that belief alone is not enough. God requires a changed life. It gets confusing doesn't it? Not really. Not if you patiently ponder the Word and simply respond as you learn. If you debate it and try to skip over verses, then it does get confusing.

Romans 8:24 says that by *hope* you shall be saved. According to that Scripture, you don't have to repent *or* believe *or* confess. All you have to do is hope. That's not the whole of truth.

The Bible says that a part of the whole truth is that you are to be baptized to be saved. It says it. That is not bad news. It's very, very good news.

Ephesians 2:8 says that by *grace* you shall be saved. That appears to say that you don't even have to hope. Does it also mean that you don't have to believe or repent or confess or be baptized. It says, "by grace you have been saved," and such is true. By grace we have been saved—not of ourselves. It is a gift of God. And we don't have one dime's worth of earning power in us to pay for our salvation.

By the grace of God, friend, there is God. We didn't do a thing to cause Him to be. By the grace of God there is the Holy Spirit, and we didn't do a thing to cause Him to be. By the grace of God there is a Savior and we didn't do a thing to cause him to be. By the grace of God there is salvation, and we didn't do a thing to cause that to be available. It is a gift from God.

People can listen to the radio, and they can listen to sermons, they can read all kinds of literature, they can come to understand that they need to believe that Jesus is the Son of God, and they can know they ought to pray to Him; but they seldom conclude that they ought to be baptized to have their sins washed away. They may be baptized to be confirmed, or to join a church, but they seldom come to the conclusion that they need to be baptized because their sins are yet to be washed away. The Scripture says you must be baptized for the removal of sin. It doesn't matter if you are fifteen or fifty-five. Sometime that has to happen. Has it?

Baptism is so important because of where it puts you . . . in Christ. The Scripture says, "Do you not know that all of us who have been buried with Christ have been baptized into His death?" We are buried with Christ. We come into contact with Jesus at that point.

Nowhere in Scripture does it say that when you believe you come into contact with Jesus. Nowhere does it say that when you confess you come into contact with Jesus. Nowhere in Scripture does it say that when you repent you come into contact with Jesus. Continually, the Scripture says that when you are baptized you come into contact with Jesus. Galatians 3:27 says that as many of you as have been baptized into Christ have been clothed with Christ.

Do you believe it? Yes.

The Lord says that in order to get rid of your sins and get into His Son, you must be baptized. In times past, God told Noah; "Get the people into the ark." Everybody who got into the ark in Noah's day was saved. Everybody outside of the ark was lost. In the New Testament we learn that everybody who gets into Jesus is saved. It doesn't matter when you were baptized to join a church. What matters is when did you get into the ark of the New Testament where you were saved? If you don't recall the day you did this, you need to consider being buried into Jesus.

Open your Bibles to Colossians Chapter 1. I want to show you something very encouraging. We are most fortunate of all people to get to hear these words. And we are most fortunate that we get to respond to them.

> We give thanks to God the Father of our Lord Jesus Christ praying always for you since we heard of your faith in Christ Jesus and the love which you have for all the saints because of the hope laid up for you in Heaven of which you previously heard in the Word of truth, the gospel which has come to you just as in all the world also it is constantly bearing fruit and increasing, even as it has been doing in you since the day you heard of it and understood the grace of God in truth (Col. 1:3).

How did they understand "the grace of God in truth"? They understood that by grace they were to be saved. And that is the truth.

In verse 13 it gets better. "For He delivered us from the domain of darkness and transferred us unto the kingdom of His beloved Son in whom we have redemption, the forgiveness of sins." God extends to us the forgiveness of sins. Look at Col. 2:9 to see *where* that forgiveness lies. "For in Him [There you have it. These people are in the ark now.] all the fullness of deity dwells in bodily form and in Him you have been made complete and He is the head over all rule and authority." Notice the repetition of the phrase, "in Him." What do you do to be saved? You get into Christ.

And in Him you were also circumcised with a circumcision made without hands in the removal of the body of the flesh by the circumcision of Christ having been buried with Him in baptism in which you were also raised up with Him through faith in the working of God who raised Him from the dead.

The people at the beginning of the book of Colossians seem to be doing so well. And they were! They were doing very well. They were bearing fruit for God because somebody sometime taught them what they needed to do to be saved. Ultimately, in chapter 2, we learn that we are baptized into Christ. Many people have been baptized into something, but have never been baptized into Christ. Satan has blocked them from the kingdom by persuading them to believe that any baptism will do. That is just not what the Scripture teaches.

If we are to have the ability to wade through

life, it will be because we were buried at sea with Christ. Romans 6 calls it a burial. The original word meant *immersion*. Really, burial in water is the only way his command can be obeyed.

Consider the three most often used methods of baptizing today: sprinkling, pouring, and immersing. The first two cannot be done to a person, only to water. One sprinkles water (on a person) or pours water (on a person), but does not sprinkle or pour the person. The third way can only be done to a person and not to water. One can immerse a person, but he certainly cannot immerse water.

Now, note the command of Jesus. "Go therefore and make disciples of all the nations, baptizing them in the name of the Father and the Son and the Holy Spirit" (Matt. 28:19). Consider again:

—You cannot sprinkle people—only water.

—You cannot pour people—only water.

—You cannot immerse water—only people.

The conclusion: Go immerse people, as people will make better disciples than water.

Buried at sea for the forgiveness of sins . . . that is how we begin to effectively wade through life!

CHAPTER SEVEN

Dare to Wade
(Wading With Motivation)

But we have this treasure in earthen vessels, that the surpassing greatness of power may be of God and not from ourselves . . . but having the same spirit of faith, according to what is written, "I believed, therefore I spoke," we also believe, therefore also we speak (2 Cor. 4:7, 13).

The inner conviction and determination to bear fruit for Christ is, at times, quenched. Intentions often get lost, dismantled, or forgotten. Contemplation without action are merely smoke signals in a land with no Indians. We have the vision to look, the imagination to dream, and the God to provide. We must have the faith to wade. Rebels in dark alleys are not the real threats to the expansion of the kingdom. Ambitious Christians with no faith to speak out grind the march to a crippled pace.

Wade. Wade by faith; not by sight. The Father can do more through His children than can be imagined (Eph. 3:20). How do we wade by faith? Consider 2 Cor. 4:7 again.

God chooses to use "earthen" vessels—you and me. We are down-to-earth, human vessels. Charles

Swindoll in his book *Improving Your Serve,* points out that God does not select the fine china or hand-painted pottery, but He chooses the chipped, scarred, and cracked, to be His ministers.

What good, good news! God does not call the somebodies, the big-names, to sow the seed. He calls everyone, including the no-names, the lonely, the suffering . . . anyone who will wade by faith! His power is perfected in weakness (2 Cor. 12:9). What a God we have, and what glory is His because of His ability to make something of our inability. The Bible abounds with teaching on His work in us.

> We have this treasure in earthen vessels, that the surpassing greatness of power may be of God and not from ourselves (2 Cor. 4:7).

> Not that we are adequate in ourselves to consider anything as coming from ourselves, but our adequacy is from God (2 Cor. 3:5).

> I planted, Apollos watered, but God was causing the growth. So then neither the one who plants nor the one who waters is anything, but God who causes the growth (1 Cor. 3: 6, 7).

> I labored even more than all of them, yet not I, but the grace of God with me (1 Cor. 15:10).

> For it is God who is at work in you (Phil. 2:13).

I can do all things through Him who strengthens me (Phil. 4:13).

(For He who effectually worked for Peter in his apostleship to the circumcised effectually worked for me also to the Gentiles) (Gal. 2:8).

. . . of which I was made a minister, according to the gift of God's grace which was given to me according to the working of His power (Eph. 3:7).

And we proclaim Him, admonishing every man and teaching every man with all wisdom, that we may present every man complete in Christ. And for this purpose also I labor, striving according to His power, which mightily works within me (Col. 1:28–29).

It is clearly that the earthen vessel—inadequate Christians combined with His might—brings about effectual labor. Countless individuals wade through life without Christ's love and guidance. Hunger for contentment is only exceeded by hunger for inner peace. Who will help? The inadequate ones must help, or else no one will.

For consider your calling, brethren, that there were not many wise according to the flesh, not many mighty, not many noble; but God has chosen the foolish things of the world to shame the wise, and God has chosen the weak things of the world to shame the things which are strong, and the base things of the world and the despised. God has chosen, the things that are not, that He might nullify the things that are, that no man should boast before God (1 Cor. 1:26–29).

When self is weak and God is strong, the spiritual combination is set for productivity that will carry an eternal weight of glory. As inadequate ones, we cannot cause growth. We are to plant and water. God causes growth. Our frailty can no more cause church growth than we can cause a bushel of apples. However, when we sow the seed, spiritual fruit will come just as surely as apples will grow by God's power once the tree has been planted. A husbandman does not cause apples. He simply sets up the conditions so that God can eventually provide a harvest.

Our role is not to be God. Our role is to be *servants*. Our concern is not how to get the sun to rise every morning, our concern is to use the sun's energy in our lives to bear fruit. It is not our concern as to how the Son will rise, it is our concern to use that Son's energy in our lives to produce spiritual fruit. Wade, inadequate one, by faith. If you have the power saw, he has the electricity to make it work.

We have bedtime stories, Bible class stories, and children's stories. Let me share with you some earthen-vessel stories!

Several years ago Jimmie Lovell conceived the idea of "going into all the world" by having English-speaking Christians correspond with people of other nations. He began to wade by faith. The results continue to be extraordinary! (Anytime you combine the ordinary with "extra" it will result in fabulous effectiveness!) Over 2,000,000 students have been contacted! More than 200,000 new students are taught each year. Over 60,000 earthen vessels wade effectively as teachers in this program. The estimated number of conversions exceeds 40,000 per year—109 baptisms per day.

All of this, by the grace of God, is happening because one man began to wade with conviction!

To make this project even more effective, Lynn Yocum established an information base for worldwide follow-ups. The World Mission Information Bank is a program of the Webb Chapel Church of Christ (13425 Webb Chapel Road, Dallas, TX 75234). They have a computer that lists most missionaries and churches of the world. It is now easier to locate a church near new students.

With your willingness to wade, you can spread the beautiful news of God to nearly all the 195 nations of the world.

You can be a part of the network of World Bible School by sending correspondence courses around the world. You'll be teaching people on the other side of the world while you sleep at night.

Here is another earthen-vessel story. Glenna Winger joined the World Bible School force. She made contact with three men in Kuara State, Nigeria. Contact was made by mail from her home in Shalimar, Florida. Those three men and sixty-six other souls were converted to the Son of God.

Samuel Young is the dean of Ghana Bible College, in Kumari, Ghana. He was baptized in 1961 after he studied the World Bible School course sent by Jerry Reynolds of Wilmington, Delaware. Recent counts indicate that an average of ten per day are being added to the church in Ghana.

Don Iverson sent one lesson to Winnie Mau of Hong Kong, China. Winnie was baptized immediately.

Darrell Foltz, a house painter from Hoxie, Kansas, became so involved in WBS that he visited Nigeria to meet some of his students. He stayed 45 days in the jungle village of Bansera. They gave him their only bed. For hours at night they would hold a lantern while Darrell read the Bible to them. He went to a nearby village, Ugep. The idol worshippers ran him out of town. The next year, this painter from Kansas returned to Ugep and converted two dozen in that wicked city.

Rama Nanda Joshi, age 23, from Kathmandu, Nepal, has received World Bible School materials for several years. Via more correspondence materials, three denominational churches were converted to the New Testament pattern. What power through earthen waders!

It is our responsibility to plant and water. Sow that seed! It isn't a burden. It's fun. Flying from Atlanta to Raleigh, North Carolina, I sat beside a lady from Red China. She spoke Chinese and English. I gave her my book, *You Can't Get to Heaven Saving Green Stamps*. She was so humble and courteous.

All I did was sow the seed. If two generations

Dare to Wade

from now her grandchildren have a garage sale they may sell that book for a nickel to the one individual whose heart is ready to seriously study the word. By faith, let's wade.

On that same airplane I saw a lady across the aisle reading. I brought out another Green Stamps book, wrote a note in it, and handed it to her across several people. In a minute the most precious note returned. We talked in the airport afterwards. She eventually took a correspondence course from her house in Cincinnati, Ohio. If we will only wade by faith.

Fausto Salvoni was born in 1907 in Rudiano, Italy. When he was 13 years old, he was sent to a Catholic seminary to be trained for the priesthood. At 21 he received his Doctors degree in Divinity and later the Masters degree in the Holy Bible. He was appointed a professor at the Catholic Seminary for Priests in Milano, Italy. Because of his scholarship, he was selected to write for the *Catholic Encyclopedia* (Vatican Edition) and the *Ecclesiastical Encyclopedia*. Other books he has written are: *The Pedagogy of the Gospels, a Bible Dictionary, A Commentary of the Book of Kings*. In the past he contributed articles to numerous Catholic magazines. Listen to his story:

> I was a Catholic priest for nineteen years (1930–1950). For nine years I taught Bible, Theology and Oriental Biblical languages in the seminary for priests at Milano, Italy. I loved the Bible and had the wonderful privilege of studying it in the original languages

at the Pontifical Biblical Institute of Rome, guided by the Jesuits. Among my teachers was the future Cardinal Bea, well known in the ecumenical movement. I tried during that time to teach the Bible faithfully and not Roman Catholic traditions. This caused me many troubles and finally obliged me to leave my teaching post.

In reality, the ultimate reason for my removal was an economical one involving a Catholic shrine. It was claimed that the house kept in the church of Loreto on the Adriatic Seashore of Italy was the home in which Mary lived in Nazareth. I taught against this. Its supposed translation by the angels through the skies is purely legend. Archaeology is against the genuineness of it. My teaching was made known to pope Pius XI who had agreed with Mussolini to exalt this sanctuary above the one at Lourdes, France, hoping to lure the pilgrims and their money into Italy rather than France. The pope was displeased with my teaching and I had to give up my lessons.

For the next ten years I worked as a parish priest in Treviglio, near Milano, in a wonderful economical position. However, I continued to study the Bible and teach it. Each year I taught in a special lectureship in Rome for Italian Bible teachers. My Bible study provoked many questions in my mind: Am I really a priest? Do I really possess the amazing power of forgiving sins in the name of God?

Can I truly change the bread of the communion into the real body of Christ and the wine into his blood? Only God knows how many nights I passed in study and prayer, reading the Bible in order to find the answers to my problems. Finally the wonderful light of truth dawned upon my mind.

In February, 1950, through personal study of the Bible, Mr. Salvoni left the Catholic church. Two years later, he was baptized for the forgiveness of sins and received the Holy Spirit. In a short time, he was preaching to large crowds of people in France, Belgium, Germany, Switzerland, Austria, Denmark, Sweden, Norway, and the United States, proclaiming his new found faith. He authored a book in the French language, entitled, *Why I Left My Priestly Robe* and another entitled, *An Ancient Priest Speaks to You.*

Fausto Salvoni directed the Bible Chair in Milano, Italy, and taught in the Bible School at Florence. He was editor of the scholarly magazine, *Biblical and Religious Research,* which is well known among Italian priests. In 1969 he was invited to the States as an Associate Professor in the Bible Department of a Christian College. In 1970 he published a work on the *History of the Papacy,* and assisted in translating the *Italian Concord Bible,* prepared jointly by Catholic, Protestant, Jewish, and Orthodox churches. He has now prepared a new modern translation of the New Testament in Italian and another large volume, *From Catholicism to Christianity.*

Now to Him who is able to do exceeding abundantly beyond all that we ask or think, according to the power that works within us (Eph. 3:20).

Dear, dear reader, considering all that He said, all that He has done and all that He can do through weak, anemic, earthen vessels like us . . .
Dare to Wade!

Test Time

At this point it may be good for you to research a few Scriptures from your Bible. "How?" and "Why?" and "What?" have been discussed. Let's search God's word. Study the following passages carefully and circle the correct answer.

1. **2 Tim. 3:16–17**
   Yes—No Did God give us *all* of the Scriptures?
   Yes—No Are the Scriptures profitable to furnish us unto all good works?
   Yes—No Do you understand this to indicate that the Bible carries authority?
   Yes—No Is the Bible a good rule book and guide for you and me?
2. **Romans 3:23**
   Yes—No Do you understand that all are guilty of sin?
3. **John 3:16**
   Yes—No Is it because of God's great love that Jesus was given so that we might live forever?
4. **Hebrews 5:8–9**

Yes—No Is Jesus the author of eternal salvation to all who *obey* Him?

Yes—No Do you agree that, although Jesus died for all men, man must obey Jesus in order that he might receive "life"?

5. John 14:6

Yes—No Is Jesus the only way to the Father?

6. Matthew 28:20

Yes—No Did Jesus say we could obey part of His will?

7. Matthew 22:37

Yes—No Must we love God in a tremendous way?

Yes—No If you love Him will you keep His commands? (John 14:15)

8. John 8:24

Yes—No Is it God's will that you believe in Jesus?

Yes—No Must you believe in Jesus to be saved?

9. Luke 13:3

Yes—No Is it God's will that you repent?

Yes—No Must you repent to have eternal life?

10. Matthew 10:32

Yes—No Is it God's will that you confess the name of Jesus before men?

Yes—No If you don't, will Jesus confess you before the Father?

11. Mark 16:15–16

Yes—No Did Jesus say, "He that believeth and is baptized shall be saved"?

Yes—No Did Jesus say, "He that believeth

shall be saved and can be baptized if he prefers"?

12. Ephesians 4:5–6
 Yes—No Is there more than one true Lord?
 Yes—No Is there more than one true baptism in God's will?

13. Acts 8:34–39
 Yes—No Did the Eunuch ask to be baptized in water?
 Yes—No Was the Eunuch taken "down *into* the water" and brought "*up out* of the water"?

14. Romans 6:3–5
 Yes—No Is baptism a burial according to the Bible?
 Yes—No Would being "baptized" like Paul and the Eunuch be a safe guide for you and me?

15. Acts 2:38
 Yes—No Was "everyone" to be baptized for the removal of sin?

16. 1 Peter 3:21
 Yes—No Does baptism save you?
 Yes—No Does baptism alone save you?
 Yes—No Does believing alone save you?
 Yes—No Does repentance alone—without believing, confessing, and being baptized—save you?

17. Ephesians 4:4
 Yes—No Does the New Testament say there is one body just as there is one Lord?

18. Ephesians 1:22–23

Yes—No   Is this one body the church?
Yes—No   Is Christ the only head of this one body?

19. 1 Corinthians 12:27
Yes—No   Are Christians Christ's body and individually members of that body?

20. Galatians 3:27
Yes—No   Does one get *into* Christ by baptism?
Yes—No   Is there any other way to get into Christ?
Yes—No   If you are in Christ are you safe?
Yes—No   If you are outside of Christ are you in danger?
Yes—No   If you are outside of Christ would you get into Him by being baptized soon?